THE F.E.A.R.L.E.S.S. BECOMING
A JOURNEY FROM FEAR TO UNSHAKEABLE FAITH

MALIKA WILLIAMS

EDITED BY
NICOLE M. QUEEN

VISION PUBLISHING
HOUSE

Vision Publishing House
support@vision-publishinghouse.com
www.vision-publishinghouse.com

ISBN: 978-1-955297-67-7 (print)

To every woman on her journey of discovering her fearless self...

Be *Encouraged*
Be *Uplifted*
Be *Empowered*

"For God has not given us a spirit of fear, but of power and of love and of a sound mind."

— 2 Timothy 1:7

CONTENTS

PREFACE

Ever since I was a young girl, fear crept in and muzzled me. I grew up in a very toxic home. My parents did the best they knew how, but they were broken and hurt, trying to raise children. This caused a lot of pain and suffering for me and my brothers. I witnessed domestic violence firsthand, where I would scream, "Please stop." In those moments, fear began to overtake me. The fear was so bad that when I heard a knock at the door, I would run and hide because I didn't know what to expect.

At the age of 8, I remember my mom packing small bags for me and my brothers and taking us to our father, who had just come home from prison and was living in a one-bedroom apartment with a woman we didn't know. She dropped us off and said, "Take your kids." This is where my first heartbreak took place. I shut down and lost all interest in being present in life. I know that what I endured in my childhood played a significant role in the decisions I made in my teenage years and early adulthood.

I got into immorality, drinking alcohol, and clubbing, which led to much disappointment and unwise decisions. It felt like a never-ending cycle. At the age of 23, I accepted the Lord as my Savior and was born again. He changed me from the inside out and helped me release all the hurt and pain I had endured from the lack of love and rejection.

I decided to stop allowing imposter syndrome to keep me in low self-esteem and became who God called me to be. I started seeing myself as an eagle, and I SOARED!

God turned what the enemy meant for evil around for my good. I was radically touched and saved at the age of 24 and rededicated my life to Christ. I then became filled with the Holy Spirit. I got married to my destiny partner, who was a promise to me from God. I didn't know I was a pastor's wife, but God does exceedingly abundantly more than we can ask or imagine.

Two years later, I was ordained as a minister and started a movement called The Fearless Becoming. I created a safe place for girls who were just like me—lost and needing to be found.

I've always had a heart for people, even as a young girl. I often wondered why I could sense when my friends needed love or when they were going through difficult times.

My journey has been one of transformation from fear to fearlessness, and it is my hope that through this book, you too will find the courage to embrace your true identity and walk boldly in your purpose. Welcome to *The Fearless Becoming*.

* * *

"She is clothed with strength and dignity, and she laughs without fear of the future." - Proverbs 31:25 (NLT)

INTRODUCTION

The Fearless Becoming is a book dedicated to guiding women from a place of fear into living fearlessly. This journey is about awakening the gifts within you and stepping into the fullness of your God-given potential. Within these pages, you will find tools and biblical solutions designed to build your self-confidence and empower you to step boldly into your mission and purpose.

"Fearless" is more than a title—it is a lifestyle and a movement that will ignite a passion within you to take action. Each chapter is crafted to empower your heart, uplift your soul, and encourage your mind. As you read, you will discover the inspiration and edification needed to equip you for your unique purpose and calling.

Throughout this book, you will be encouraged to embrace a life free from fear, anchored in the love and power of Christ. We will explore practical steps and spiritual insights that will help you overcome obstacles and break free from the chains of insecurity and doubt. You will learn to trust in the Lord's promises and lean into His unwavering support.

This is your moment to embrace everything our Abba Father has placed within you and to let your light shine brightly. Be inspired to live fearlessly and to build your identity firmly on Christ. You are called to be a beacon of hope and strength, influencing those around you with the grace and power of the Holy Spirit.

As you journey through this book, remember to have faith. You are established in Christ; every word spoken over your life will be accomplished. You are the righteousness of God, born to be legendary. Embrace the process of evolving, knowing that sanctification is your portion. Always maintain your self-confidence, knowing that you are equipped and empowered by the Almighty God.

In *The Fearless Becoming,* you will find a roadmap to a transformed life, where fear is replaced with boldness, uncertainty with clarity, and insecurity with unwavering confidence. This is your invitation to walk boldly and courageously into your mission and purpose, knowing that you are supported by a loving Father who has destined you for greatness.

Let this book be a catalyst for your fearless becoming. Allow it to stir up the gifts within you, to challenge you, and to propel you into the extraordinary life God has prepared for you. Embrace this journey with an open heart, ready to receive the fullness of what God has in store.

Welcome to *The Fearless Becoming.* Your transformation starts now.

I

"F" IS FOR FAITH

THE FOUNDATION OF HOPE

Faith is the cornerstone of our hope and the bedrock of our spiritual journey. As Hebrews 11:6 reminds us, "And without faith, it is impossible to please God." To achieve our dreams and aspirations, we must first believe in their possibility. Faith acts as a catalyst, transforming our desires into reality.

FAITH: THE CURRENCY OF GOD

Faith is the currency of God. It is this divine currency that removes roadblocks and flattens mountains. Even the smallest measure of faith, as tiny as a mustard seed, holds immense power. This seemingly insignificant amount is enough to propel you into your destined place, to birth the vision God has placed within you, and to fulfill the divine plan for your life.

THE JOURNEY OF FAITH

In the most challenging seasons, faith serves as an anchor. When circumstances seem insurmountable, unwavering belief is what carries one through. During times when everything seems to be falling apart, it is faith that keeps one hopeful, convinced that God has more in store. This belief doesn't just sustain; it moves God.

A BIBLICAL PERSPECTIVE ON FAITH

The Bible is replete with stories that underscore the power of faith. John 20:29 tells us, "Because you have seen me, you have believed. Blessed are those who have not seen, and yet have believed." This verse highlights the essence of faith—believing without seeing. It's this kind of faith that God honors and responds to.

FAITH IN ACTION

Faith is not passive; it requires action. James 2:17 states, "In the same way, faith by itself, if it is not accompanied by action, is dead." True faith compels us to move forward, to take steps even when the path is unclear. It's about trusting God's promises and acting on them.

FAITH: AN ASSET FOR GROWTH

Faith is indispensable for spiritual growth. It breaks barriers and dismantles strongholds in your life. With faith, you can overcome any obstacle and achieve what God has set before you.

PRACTICAL STEPS TO STRENGTHEN YOUR FAITH

1. *Prayer and Meditation:* Regularly communicate with God through prayer. Meditate on His promises and let them sink deep into your heart.

2. *Study the Word:* Immerse yourself in the Bible. The stories of faith found within its pages will inspire and strengthen your own beliefs.
3. *Surround Yourself with Believers:* Fellowship with other believers who can encourage and support you in your faith journey.
4. *Act on Your Faith:* Take practical steps towards your goals, trusting that God will guide and provide for you.

* * *

Heavenly Father, I pray that our faith will not fail us. Lord, may there be a divine connection between our faith and our works that produces great results in our walk with You. Stretch our faith to new levels that move mountains and tear down walls. Father, as we hear Your Word, let faith be activated in us like never before. Increase our ability to withstand trials as we contend for breakthroughs. *In Jesus' mighty name, Amen.*

2

"E" IS FOR ESTABLISH

YOUR PURPOSE HAS BEEN ESTABLISHED

Your purpose was established long before the foundations of the earth. Ephesians 1:4 states, "Even as he chose us in him before the foundation of the world, that we should be holy and blameless before him in love." Reflect on this for a moment: you were brought into this world with a specific purpose. You were a thought before you were a seed.

GOD'S PLAN FOR YOU

Our Father created you for a specific assignment, and as Jeremiah 29:11 assures us, it is not to harm you but to give you hope and a future. Everything that pertains to you has been established in heaven, and it is our responsibility to bring heaven down to earth concerning our lives.

THE POWER OF PRAYER

Prayer is a powerful tool that connects us to the Father, allowing us to receive divine intel, revelation, wisdom, knowledge, and understanding. It is through prayer that He reveals who we truly are. This divine communion anchors us in Him, helping us understand our established purpose.

THE ROLE OF FASTING

Fasting is essential in breaking the yokes of bondage that hinder our walk with Christ and delay the promises of God in our lives. Isaiah 58:6 declares, "Is not this the kind of fasting I have chosen: to loose the chains of injustice and untie the cords of the yoke, to set the oppressed free and break every yoke?" Fasting destroys the chains that keep us stagnant, enabling us to move forward in our divine purpose.

REFLECT ON YOUR ESTABLISHED PLACE

Since we desire to fulfill our God-given assignments, and knowing that we are already established in Him, I pose this question to you: How have you operated in your established place?

PRACTICAL STEPS TO OPERATE IN YOUR ESTABLISHED PLACE

1. *Seek God's Guidance:* Regularly seek God's direction through prayer and meditation on His word. Ask Him to reveal your purpose and guide your steps.
2. *Engage in Fasting:* Incorporate fasting into your spiritual routine to break free from any bondage and gain clarity on your divine assignment.
3. *Study the Scriptures:* Dive deep into the Bible to understand

God's promises and plans for you. Let His words affirm your established purpose.

4. *Surround Yourself with Support:* Engage with a community of believers who can encourage you and hold you accountable as you walk in your purpose.

5. *Take Action:* Begin to take practical steps towards fulfilling your purpose. Whether it's through ministry, work, or personal endeavors, act on what God has revealed to you.

* * *

Lord, I pray that each person who reads this book will come to know their purpose. Father, speak to them even now concerning who they are. Reveal their purpose through divine intelligence in the name of Jesus. For You have said that Your plans are not of evil or harm but to give us a hope and a future. Father, I believe that as they read this, they will discover their true identity in You. Enable them to see far beyond what they can see with the natural eye. Release them, Father, into their purpose. *In Jesus' name, Amen.*

3

"A" IS FOR ACCOMPLISH

FULFILLING DIVINE PROMISES

That which has been spoken over your life shall accomplish what it was sent out to do. We are capable of achieving anything we set our minds to. With the help of the Holy Spirit, our minds become powerful tools to create the life we desire. However, transformation requires the renewal of our minds, as stated in Romans 12:2: "Do not conform to the pattern of this world, but be transformed by the renewing of your mind."

THE PATH TO ACCOMPLISHMENT

To accomplish great things and achieve success, we must not conform to the world's patterns. Accomplishments require dedication, hard work, sacrifice, and diligence. The good news is that we are empowered by the grace of God to do all things.

EMPOWERED BY GRACE

Scriptures like 1 John 4:4, "Greater is He that is in you than he that is in the world," offer profound encouragement. This truth edifies the soul, reminding us that while our spirit is willing, it is often our flesh that is weak. Therefore, it is crucial to immerse ourselves in the Word of God to transform our dreams into accomplishments.

LEARNING FROM JESUS

Jesus accomplished and fulfilled the scriptures, setting the ultimate example. He demonstrated that we, too, are called to perform greater exploits. By following His example, we can achieve the desires that are deep within our hearts.

PRACTICAL STEPS TO ACCOMPLISH YOUR GOALS

1. *Renew Your Mind:* Engage in regular study and meditation on the Word of God to transform your thinking and align it with divine purposes.
2. *Dedicate Yourself:* Commit to your goals with dedication and hard work. Understand that accomplishments require sacrifice and perseverance.
3. *Rely on God's Grace:* Depend on the grace of God to empower and guide you. Remember that it is through His strength that you can do all things.
4. *Stay Encouraged:* Read and meditate on scriptures that reinforce your faith and encourage your spirit. Let the Word of God be your constant source of motivation.
5. *Take Action:* Faith without works is dead. Put in the necessary effort to back up your faith and bring your dreams to fruition.

* * *

Heavenly Father, Thank You for Your Word that never returns void but accomplishes what You desire and achieves the purpose for which You sent it. We are grateful for the promises fulfilled and the guidance Your Word provides. Lord, let Your Word continue to transform our lives, bringing wisdom, strength, and direction. May we hold steadfastly to Your truths, knowing that Your Word is a firm foundation. Thank You for the power of Your accomplished Word in our lives. We celebrate the changes and breakthroughs it brings, and we look forward to the continued work it will do in us and through us. *In Jesus' name, Amen.*

4

"R" IS FOR RIGHTEOUS

THE RIGHTEOUSNESS OF GOD

You are the righteousness of God. The Lord holds a special love for righteous women—those who are not only faithful but filled with faith. These women are optimistic and cheerful because they know who they are and where they are going. They strive to live and serve as women of God, upholding standards of morality, justice, and virtue.

PRACTICAL STEPS TO CULTIVATE THE VIRTUES OF A RIGHTEOUS WOMAN

- *Faith*: Faith is the most important virtue. The Prophet Joseph Smith taught that faith in the Lord Jesus Christ is "the foundation of all righteousness." Striving to live the commandments allows faith to grow. In exercising faith, one becomes cheerful, optimistic, charitable, and courageous, as faith is the moving cause of all these virtues.

- *Honesty*: Honesty begins with oneself. To be honest with others, one must first be honest internally. This integrity forms the basis of trust and righteousness.

- *Chastity*: The sacred powers of procreation are intended to be exercised only within the bounds of marriage, as stated in "The Family: A Proclamation to the World." Intimacy outside of marriage leads to guilt and emotional hurt, whereas within marriage, it brings joy and happiness. Chastity before marriage and fidelity after marriage are key to self-respect and fulfillment.

- *Humility*: Humility is about balance. Receiving compliments graciously without letting them inflate one's ego is a mark of humility. A humble person is teachable, and the Lord promises enlightenment to the humble and contrite. Admitting when one doesn't know something is a sign of true humility.

- *Self-Discipline:* Self-discipline is crucial for achieving goals and developing character. Habits formed through self-discipline in youth become part of one's character for life. Discipline in work and personal habits is imperative for success and is a testament to being a disciple of Christ.

- *Fairness*: Fairness and compassion in dealings with others reflect the teachings of Jesus. The parable of the unjust servant illustrates the importance of showing the same compassion we have received. Fairness ensures that one is just in their interactions, fostering mutual respect.

- *Moderation*: Practicing moderation in all things, except those expressly forbidden by the Lord, is wise. Avoiding extremes in dress, behavior, and lifestyle aligns with the spirit of the

Word of Wisdom. Ephesians 5:18 advises against excess and encourages being filled with the Holy Spirit instead.

- *Cleanliness*: Cleanliness in dress and appearance is essential. The current age may lean towards sloppy dress and manners, but maintaining cleanliness and modesty reflects respect for oneself and others. Personal cleanliness and neatness are important virtues.

- Courage: Courage is needed to stand against peer pressure, resist temptation, withstand ridicule, and uphold the truth. Life's challenges require courage to persevere and maintain faith. Isaiah 41:10 offers assurance: "Fear not, I am with thee; oh, be not dismayed, for I am thy God and will still give thee aid. I'll strengthen thee, help thee, and cause thee to stand, upheld by my righteous, omnipotent hand."

- *Grace*: Growing in grace, as advised in the Doctrine and Covenants, is about kindness and goodness. Grace is a charming trait that combines personal dignity and inner beauty. Cheerfulness and a pleasing appearance stem from self-worth and grace, making one attractive in character and spirit.

* * *

Father, I pray for every woman reading this that this is the time our devotion to You deepens. Thank You that we willingly seek You, desiring and looking for times to stay in Your presence. We are disciples committed to following You in all Your ways. Lord, we are ready to commit to a devoted study, a devoted prayer life, and a devoted fasting life. In this commitment, we will experience more of Your power, grace, and strength because we are fully submitted to You in obedience and surrender. *In Jesus' name, Amen.*

5

"L" IS FOR LEGENDARY

EMBRACING YOUR LEGENDARY STATUS

You are fit to be a legend. For true believers, loyalty is demonstrated through unwavering commitment to Jesus and His gospel. As Mark 8:35 and Romans 1:16 highlight, loyalty involves acknowledging Jesus Christ as our sole source of authority and salvation (Matthew 28:18; John 14:6).

THE DEVOTION OF A DISCIPLE

Such devotion and commitment should reflect the attitude of the apostle Peter, who said, "If anyone speaks, he should do it as one speaking the very words of God. If anyone serves, he should do it with the strength God provides, so that in all things God may be praised through Jesus Christ" (1 Peter 4:11).

LOYALTY AND SELF-SACRIFICE

As disciples of Jesus, loyalty and self-sacrificing allegiance are key. This involves following His command: "If anyone would come after

Me, he must deny himself and take up his cross and follow Me" (Mark 8:34). Even when we falter in our loyalty, we have the assurance of His steadfast presence: "And surely I am with you always, even to the very end of the age" (Matthew 28:20b).

PRACTICAL STEPS TO CULTIVATE LEGENDARY VIRTUES

1. *Commit to Jesus' Teachings:* Make a daily commitment to study and follow Jesus' teachings. Let His words guide your actions and decisions.
2. *Acknowledge His Authority:* Recognize Jesus as the ultimate authority in your life. Submit your plans and desires to His will.
3. *Live with Integrity:* Speak and act as if representing God in all things, just as 1 Peter 4:11 advises. Let your integrity shine in every aspect of your life.
4. *Serve with Strength:* Utilize the strength God provides to serve others. Whether in your community, church, or family, let your service bring glory to God.
5. *Deny Self and Follow Christ:* Embrace the call to deny yourself, take up your cross, and follow Jesus. This means prioritizing His will above personal comfort and desires.
6. *Stay Faithful in Trials:* Remain steadfast in your loyalty to Christ, especially during challenging times. Trust that He is with you always, providing strength and guidance.
7. *Reflect His Love:* Show the love of Christ in your interactions. Be a beacon of His compassion and grace to those around you.
8. *Seek Continuous Growth:* Regularly seek spiritual growth through prayer, worship, and fellowship with other believers. Aim to deepen your relationship with Christ continually.
9. *Embrace Assurance:* Hold on to the promise that Jesus is with

you always. Let this assurance give you confidence and peace in your journey.

10. *Be a Living Testimony:* Let your life be a testimony to God's faithfulness. Share your journey and experiences to inspire and encourage others.

* * *

O Almighty God, We come before You in awe and reverence, acknowledging Your greatness and sovereignty. You are the Creator of all things, the source of all wisdom and strength. We seek Your guidance and blessing as we strive for excellence and honor in our endeavors. Grant us the courage to pursue our dreams with unwavering faith and the wisdom to navigate challenges with integrity. May our efforts be marked by perseverance, and our successes reflect Your glory. Help us to inspire and uplift those around us, becoming beacons of hope and encouragement. Empower us, Lord, to leave a lasting legacy that honors You. Let our actions and achievements serve as testimonies of Your goodness and grace. In all that we do, may we seek to bring glory to Your name. *In Jesus' mighty name, we pray. Amen.*

6

"E" IS FOR EVOLVE

EMBRACING EVOLUTION IN CHRIST

Dominating is in your DNA. As believers, we are called to continuously evolve in our faith and walk with Christ. To evolve in Christ is to continuously grow and be transformed by His presence in our lives. By staying rooted in Him and building upon our faith, we can live a life that reflects His glory and purpose. Colossians 2:6-7 encourages us: "So then, just as you received Christ Jesus as Lord, continue to live in Him, rooted and built up in Him, strengthened in the faith as you were taught, and overflowing with thankfulness."

LIVING IN CHRIST

To evolve means to grow and develop continually in Christ. This involves being deeply rooted and built up in Him, allowing our faith to be strengthened as we overflow with thankfulness. Our journey is one of constant growth and transformation.

PRACTICAL STEPS TO EVOLVE IN YOUR FAITH

1. *Stay Rooted and Build on Your Foundation:* Ensure your faith is deeply rooted in Jesus by immersing yourself in prayer and scripture. Continuously build on this foundation through study, worship, and fellowship.
2. *Strengthen and Apply Your Faith:* Engage in spiritual disciplines, seek wisdom from mentors, and participate in community worship to strengthen your faith. Put your faith into action by serving others, sharing the gospel, and living out Christ's teachings.
3. *Embrace Challenges and Continuous Learning:* View challenges as opportunities for growth. Trust that God uses every situation to refine your character. Never stop learning—attend Bible studies, read books, and listen to teachings that deepen your understanding of God's word.
4. *Cultivate Thankfulness and Reflect on Your Journey:* Overflow with thankfulness in all circumstances to keep your focus on God's goodness. Regularly reflect on your spiritual journey, acknowledge your progress, and set new goals for continued growth.
5. *Surround Yourself with Support and Be Open to Change:* Engage with a community of believers who encourage and support your evolution in faith. Embrace changes that come with growth, being willing to let go of old habits and mindsets that no longer serve your walk with Christ.

* * *

Heavenly Father, Thank You for the transformation taking place in our lives. Your presence transforms us, and in Your presence, there is fullness of joy. May our lives reflect Your glory. Rooted and grounded in You, thankfulness flows from our hearts. Thank You for Your grace as we continually evolve into who we are truly called to be. Prepare our hearts for change and fill us with expectation for the great things ahead and for who we are becoming. *In Jesus' name, Amen.*

7

"S" IS FOR SANCTIFICATION

EMBRACING SANCTIFICATION

Sanctification is the process of being made holy, a work of God
within us. As believers, our bodies are the temple of God, and through
sanctification, we become more like Christ. Paul highlights the Holy
Spirit's essential role in this process, as seen in Galatians 5:16,18,25,
where he repeatedly uses the phrase "by the Spirit." Romans 15:16 also
emphasizes that we are "sanctified by the Holy Spirit," and in Romans
8:13, Paul states that it is "by the Spirit" that we can "put to death the
deeds of the body."

THE ROLE OF THE HOLY SPIRIT

Sanctification is a divine work accomplished by the Holy Spirit in the
lives of believers. It is deeply intertwined in the work of the Holy
Spirit, as He guides, empowers, and transforms us, enabling us to live
holy lives that reflect God's nature. By recognizing our bodies as
God's temple and depending on the Holy Spirit, we can actively
participate in this transformative process. Embrace the journey of

becoming more like Christ, knowing that it is "by the Spirit" that we are made holy.

PRACTICAL STEPS TO EMBRACE SANCTIFICATION

1. *Acknowledge and Respect Your Body:* Recognize your body as the temple of the Holy Spirit. Treat it with care and honor, understanding its sacred nature.
2. *Depend on the Holy Spirit:* Seek the Holy Spirit's strength and guidance daily. Allow Him to lead your decisions and actions.
3. *Commit to Spiritual Growth:* Engage in spiritual practices like prayer, Bible study, and worship to deepen your relationship with God.
4. *Strive for Holiness:* Actively work to avoid sin and pursue righteousness. Let the Holy Spirit help you overcome sinful behaviors.
5. *Engage with Scripture and Community:* Regularly meditate on scriptures about sanctification and holiness. Surround yourself with a supportive community of believers.
6. *Practice Self-Discipline and Patience:* Develop self-discipline in areas of needed change. Be patient with yourself, recognizing that sanctification is a gradual process.
7. *Celebrate Your Progress:* Acknowledge and celebrate your progress in your sanctification journey. Give glory to God for every step forward.

* * *

Heavenly Father, We come before You in humble adoration, seeking Your presence and grace. Purify our hearts and minds, washing us clean from all unrighteousness. Fill us with Your Holy Spirit, that we may walk in Your ways and reflect Your love and holiness in all we do.x

Transform our lives, Lord, making us more like Christ each day. Strengthen us to resist temptation and to live in obedience to Your Word. May our actions, thoughts, and words be pleasing to You, and may we be vessels of Your peace and love to those around us. Guide us, Lord, in Your truth, and sanctify us through and through. We dedicate ourselves to You, trusting in Your power to make us holy as You are holy. *In Jesus' name, we pray. Amen.*

8

"S" IS FOR SELF-CONFIDENT

EMBRACING GOD-COMMANDED CONFIDENCE

Confidence is a commandment of God. As stated in Joshua 1:9, "Have I not commanded you? Be strong and courageous." Hebrews 10:35-36 reinforces this, saying, "Do not throw away your confidence; it will be richly rewarded. You need to persevere so that when you have done the will of God, you will receive what He has promised."

THE POWER OF CONFIDENCE

Your success will be determined by your own confidence and fortitude. When we are motivated and confident in our abilities, we develop the strength to face all the challenges in our lives. Confidence is not just a trait but a God-given command to trust in the abilities and strength He has vested in us. This God-given confidence will empower you to achieve success and fulfill His purposes for your life.

PRACTICAL STEPS TO CULTIVATE SELF-CONFIDENCE

1. *Trust in God's Promises*: Believe in the promises of God. Let His Word be the foundation of your confidence. Know that He has equipped you with everything you need to succeed.
2. *Be Courageous:* Embrace the command to be strong and courageous. Face your fears and challenges head-on, knowing that God is with you.
3. *Persevere Through Challenges:* Develop fortitude by persevering through difficult times. Remember that perseverance is key to receiving what God has promised.
4. *Acknowledge Your Strengths:* Recognize and celebrate the abilities and strengths God has given you. Use them boldly to fulfill His purposes.
5. *Stay Motivated:* Keep your motivation high by setting goals and reminding yourself of God's faithfulness. Let His promises drive you forward.
6. *Speak Positively:* Affirm yourself with positive and faith-filled words. Speak God's truth over your life and reject any negative thoughts.
7. *Surround Yourself with Encouragement:* Be around people who uplift and encourage you. Their support will help reinforce your confidence.
8. *Prepare and Plan:* Equip yourself with knowledge and skills. Being well-prepared boosts your confidence in handling various situations.
9. *Learn from Failures:* See failures as learning opportunities. Each setback is a chance to grow and improve, not a reason to lose confidence.
10. *Reflect on Past Successes:* Remind yourself of past victories and how God.

* * *

Heavenly Father, Thank You for rooting our hearts in Your unwavering love, so we will not be shaken or moved. Help us to understand that our identity is solely built in You and nothing else. Let us hold fast to our confidence, not losing ourselves in the midst of evolving. Keep us from putting on masks or adopting false identities. May we fully embrace who You have made us to be, confident that He who began a good work in us will complete it. Thank You, Father, that we are not orphans but fully accepted and loved by You. We are grateful for the transformation You have made available to us. Guide us to walk boldly in this new identity and continue to evolve. *In Jesus' name. Amen.*

A Letter from Lady Malika

Being a daughter of the Most High God comes with so many benefits. The Bible says daily He loads us up with benefits (Psalm 68:19). As a daughter, you want to feel a daddy's hug, love, and hear his encouraging kind words. Many daughters have not heard kind words from their biological dad or have felt any affection from a biological dad. What I can say about our Father in heaven is that He loves well. He loves with an everlasting love that can pick you up from any deep pit or dark place you find yourself in.

The enemy wants us to believe a fake identity he made up, but in Christ, our spirits have a perfect identity. Identity is important; it's the foundation. Walk it out as a daughter. Walk into your identity as a co-heir with Christ Jesus.

We're called to pour into others, to mentor, and to be a spiritual mother to those the Father assigns to us.

The Word of God in 2 Corinthians 6:14 states: "Be ye not unequally yoked together with unbelievers: for what fellowship hath righteousness with unrighteousness? and what communion hath light with darkness?" So, who are you teaming up with? Are you aware of who you are yoked with? Don't team up with those who are unbelievers. Partner with those who come alongside you and encourage you.

You are carrying the authority of Christ. Our Father is Royalty; He is the Lord of Lords and the King of Kings. Therefore, because we are made in His image and likeness, we are royalty. The Word of God in 1 Peter 2:9 says, "But you are a chosen generation, a royal priesthood, a holy nation, His own special people, that you may proclaim the praises of Him who called you out of darkness into His marvelous light." Know that as a daughter of God, you have the right to receive a special reward which can be translated into unmerited favor, which means preferential favor—the preferred ones. You have been chosen by God as a preferred daughter to be great in the land of the living.

As a daughter of God, our Father wants to establish our true identity and make it clear to us. The Father's assignment is to instill our identity. It is the father who imparts the seed and the mother who carries the seed in her womb. The seed comes from the father because the father has the ability to provide the child's identity. You have been given a special identity through your Daddy in heaven. Please read Psalm 139. My favorite scripture in the passage is verse 14: "I am fearfully and wonderfully made; this I know full well."

When you know who you are, you are able to reach things that you never knew you had the ability to reach. My identity was restored when I gave my life to Christ. I used to be fearful and afraid to step out on my dreams because I feared what people would think. I was in a constant state of fear and always felt rejected because that's all I knew. When I decided to say, "Lord, here I am. Search me, oh Lord," and read His Word, the scripture changed my life. It was the love of God that shifted the way I viewed myself. The love of God is not like worldly love; His love is unwavering and it's consistent. When you feel that kind of love, you will want to identify with Him even more, and then the transformation begins to become not just a speech but an experience.

I pray that through this, God will reveal just how much He loves you and how special you truly are. You are worthy and capable of doing all things through Christ who gives you strength (Philippians 4:13).

With love,

Lady Malika Williams

PROPHECY FOR THE DAUGHTERS OF YESHUA

The weight of my glory is falling upon you; it will be heavy. The winds of acceleration are coming. With these mantles, there will be an ushering in of a greater momentum of the Lord's Spirit. Where the enemy tried to steal your momentum, the Lord is realigning you.

Strength or force is coming upon you to do what the Lord has called you to do. You will find that you have energy, power, strength, and drive. You will no longer compare yourself to others and look down upon yourself. The Lord is delivering the daughters from the orphan spirit.

It's time to come up higher. It's time to stop entertaining negative self-talk and talk with the King. Yes, the Father is ready to refine and replenish.

There is a strong alignment happening for those of us who have stayed the course. Many of my daughters are about to pick back up the assignments you dropped. New mantles are being released to my daughters.

Build in a greater measure and go deeper in your love for the Lord. Discernment is key for the new doors. Know what the Lord is saying. John 10:7: "I am the door; by me if any man enters in, he shall be saved, and shall go in and out, and find pasture."

PRAYER TO RESTORE IDENTITY

Father, in the name of Jesus, I pray as Your daughter for a baptism of love for the women who have read this book. Father, I thank You for restoring them to the original intent of their lives before the foundation of the world.

Lord, we know that many have been heartbroken, disappointed, rejected, and betrayed; however, Your word says that You are close to the brokenhearted according to Psalm 34:18. Father, we pray that You would mend every broken piece into one whole, and healthy heart.

May Your daughters experience joy for their tears and praise for their heaviness in the name of Jesus. Father, we thank You for their true identity being revealed to them.

Thank You for the passion that leads to purpose being ignited in them. Lord, we bless You for the full recompense of what the enemy has stolen. He must return everything back sevenfold in the mighty name of Jesus.

Thank You, Father, that this prayer is sealed under the blood of Jesus and it shall accomplish what it was sent out to do. In Jesus' name, Amen.

ACKNOWLEDGMENTS

I would like to take a moment to express my deepest gratitude to all the incredible ladies who have supported me every step of the way. Your unwavering belief in me, even when I struggled to believe in myself, has been a constant source of strength. Every word of encouragement, every prophecy, and all your prayers and dedication to my growth have profoundly impacted my journey. I am truly honored to be connected to each one of you. You stood by me as I was figuring out who I was, and for that, I appreciate and love you all.

Thank you to my wonderful family—my husband and children. Your patience and support have allowed me the time to pursue this goal, and your love has been a foundation I could always rely on. I am deeply grateful for every way in which you have supported me.

To the leaders who have been a part of my growth and impartation, thank you for your guidance and mentorship. A special shout-out to Apostle David and Tracy Whittington: your love and support during a low point in my life, without judgment but with genuine care, has meant the world to me.

From the bottom of my heart, thank you to everyone who has played a significant role in my journey. Your impact on my life is immeasurable.

ABOUT THE AUTHOR

Lady Malika Williams is a native of Baltimore, Maryland, who was raised in a broken and dysfunctional environment. For many years, she searched for a safe place and eventually surrendered to the love of God, who gave her a new identity and unfailing grace in Christ.

She accepted Christ and was filled with the Holy Spirit at "More Than Conquerors Worldwide Inc." There, she faithfully attended and was quickly transformed, receiving the Holy Spirit with the evidence of a new lifestyle and language. Through humility, she was shaped and molded by God, leading to the birth of her organization, Fearless Women On Rise LLC. This venture includes holistic skincare products, t-shirts, and counseling services.

Lady Malika serves in ministry alongside her husband and their blended family of seven beautiful children. She is a sought-after ordained minister and an anointed preacher. She is currently pioneering a virtual community called Fearless Nation and oversees the HEAL The Broken Women group on Facebook. Additionally, she mentors preteen young ladies and serves as a mother to many.

Guided by her life scripture, Proverbs 31:25, "She is clothed with strength and dignity; she can laugh at the days to come," Lady Malika Williams is dedicated to helping women find their voice and identity.

* * *

To get in touch with Lady Malika, please contact her here:
Email: womenfearless@gmail.com

www.ingramcontent.com/pod-product-compliance
Lightning Source LLC
Chambersburg PA
CBHW051554120626
46551CB00013B/1513